GIOACCHINO ROSSINI

PETITE MESSE SOLENNELLE

FÜR VIER SOLOSTIMMEN, CHOR
HARMONIUM UND KLAVIER

HERAUSGEGEBEN VON
ANDREAS SCHENCK

C. F. PETERS · FRANKFURT

LEIPZIG · LONDON · NEW YORK

INHALT

Erster Teil

Zweiter Teil

Aufführungsdauer: ca. 90 Min.

Vorwort

Gioacchino Rossini (1792–1868) ist als Komponist geistlicher Werke nie recht in das Bewußtsein der musikalischen Öffentlichkeit getreten. Tatsächlich ist die Zahl der Kirchenkompositionen, gemessen an seinem Opernschaffen, gering. Jedoch gehören die zwei großen geistlichen Kompositionen, das *Stabat Mater* und die *Petite Messe solennelle*, zu seinen bedeutendsten Werken, und gerade letztere ist von besonderer Originalität. Die Messe entstand lange nach Rossinis Rückzug von der Oper. Sie ist die umfangreichste Komposition der zweiten Lebenshälfte und sein letztes größeres Werk.

Rossini begann mit der Komposition 1863, im Alter von 71 Jahren. Anlaß für die Uraufführung am 14. März 1864 war die Einweihung der Hauskapelle des Grafen und der Gräfin Pillet-Will, die zu Rossinis Freundeskreis in Paris zählten; das Werk ist der Gräfin gewidmet. Die kleine Besetzung für vier Soli, Doppelquartett, zwei Klaviere und Harmonium entsprach dem privaten Rahmen der Veranstaltung, die unter Ausschluß der Öffentlichkeit stattfand. In der handschriftlichen Partitur findet sich der folgende Vermerk: *„Petite Messe solennelle, für vier Stimmen mit Begleitung von zwei Klavieren und Harmonium, die während meines Aufenthaltes auf dem Lande in Passy komponiert wurde. Zwölf Sänger der drei Geschlechter – Männer, Frauen und Castrati – genügen für ihre Aufführung, das heißt acht für den Chor und vier für die Soli, im ganzen zwölf Cherubim."* Der Hinweis auf die „drei Geschlechter" ist sicherlich nicht ganz ernst zu nehmen. Zu jener Zeit gab es bereits keine Kastraten mehr, jedoch hatte Rossini in seiner Jugend ihre Kunst sehr bewundert und die spätere Entwicklung des Gesanges immer pessimistischer beurteilt. So ironisch seine Bemerkung scheint – aus ihr spricht die Sehnsucht nach einem vergangenen Gesangsideal und damit eine ganz bestimmte Klangvorstellung. Das Instrumentarium, Harmonium und Klavier, war zu jener Zeit in Frankreich nicht ungewöhnlich; auch Lesueur, Gounod und Franck haben geistliche Werke für Klavier und Orgel bzw. Harmonium geschrieben. Nach der erfolgreichen Uraufführung erstellte Rossini auf Drängen seiner Freunde eine Orchesterfassung, durch die die Messe einem breiteren Publikum bekannt wurde; gegen die Originalbesetzung hat sie sich jedoch auf Dauer nicht durchsetzen können. Heute wird allerdings der zweite Klavierpart, der lediglich zur Verstärkung bestimmter Passagen diente, üblicherweise in die erste Klavierstimme integriert; so auch in der vorliegenden Ausgabe.

Das Beiwort „petite" im Titel bezieht sich nur auf die Besetzung; mit einer Länge von über 80 Minuten ist die Messe alles andere als klein. Ihre vierzehn Nummern enthalten den vollständigen Meßtext; zusätzlich fügte Rossini den Hymnus *O salutaris hostia* ein. Die Bedeutung des Werkes liegt im Reichtum der musikalischen Gestaltung, in der Leggerezza der Melodien und der spielerischen Leichtigkeit im Umgang mit dem „gelehrten" Stil der Kirchenmusik. Gerade dieses mag Rossini ein Anliegen gewesen sein; er, der im Kontrapunkt nur wenig ausgebildet worden war und unter anderem von Beethoven den Rat erhielt, bei der Oper zu bleiben und „viele Barbiere" zu schreiben, setzte in seinem letzten Werk besonderen Ehrgeiz in der Verarbeitung tradierter Formen der geistlichen Musik. So ist der a cappella auszuführende *Christe*-Teil des *Kyrie* eine Reminiszenz an die altklassische Vokalpolyphonie der Palestrina-Zeit. Die glänzenden Doppelfugen des *Gloria* und des *Credo* sind vom Geiste des „Stile antico" inspiriert, und die Beschäftigung mit Bach fand ihren Niederschlag im instrumentalen *Preludio religioso*. Die Tiefe des Ausdrucks einerseits und die ironische Brechung auf der anderen Seite erscheinen als das eigenartigste Charakteristikum dieser Messe. Die Tempobezeichnung „Allegro Cristiano" im *Credo*, die hüpfende Klavierbegleitung der Chorfugen verraten den augenzwinkernden Spötter, während andere Teile wie etwa das *Kyrie* und das *Agnus Dei* von bezwingender Ernsthaftigkeit sind. Bei aller Vielfalt bleibt die Geschlossenheit des Werkes gewahrt. Die Nummernfolge innerhalb der großen Abschnitte *Gloria* und *Credo* ist durch Wiederholungen verknüpft, und auch weiträumige harmonischen Entsprechungen wie etwa zu Beginn von *Gloria* und *Sanctus* zeugen von der formalen Durchgestaltung der Messe.

Sein musikalisches Vermächtnis begleitete Rossini mit den folgenden Sätzen, die in der Originalpartitur enthalten sind: *„Lieber Gott, da ist sie, die arme kleine Messe. Ist es heilige Musik (musique sacree), die ich geschrieben habe, oder verfluchte Musik (sacree musique)? Ich bin für die Opera buffa geschaffen, wie Du genau weißt. Ein bißchen Können, ein bißchen Herz, das ist alles. Sei denn gepriesen und laß mich ins Paradies. G. Rossini. Passy 1863."*

Christiane a Campo

Foreword

Gioacchino Rossini (1792–1868) has never truly entered the consciousness of the musical public as a composer of sacred music. Indeed, the number of his ecclesiastical compositions is slight, compared with his operatic oeuvres. Nevertheless, two great sacred compositions, the *Stabat mater* and the *Petite messe solennelle*, are among his most significant works and the latter is of particular originality. The Mass was composed long after Rossini's retirement from opera. It is the most extensive composition from the second half of his life and his last major work.

Rossini began the composition in 1863, at the age of 71. The occasion of the première on March 14 1864 was the consecration of the private chapel of Count and Countess Pillet-Will, who numbered among Rossini's circle of friends in Paris; the work is dedicated to the Countess. The small orchestration for four soloists, double quartet, two pianos and harmonium was in keeping with the private setting of the event, which took place to the exclusion of the public. The following annotation is found in the manuscript score: *„Petite messe solennelle, for four voices with the accompaniment of two pianos and harmonium, which was composed in Passy during my sojourn in the country. Twelve singers of three sexes – men, women and castrati – will suffice for its performance; that is, eight for the choir and the four soloists, making twelve cherubim in all.“* The reference to „three sexes“ is certainly not to be taken entirely seriously. At that time there were no longer any castrati, yet in his youth Rossini had greatly admired their artistry and viewed the future development of singing increasingly pessimistically. As ironic as his remark appears, it speaks of the longing for a bygone ideal of singing and with it a very special concept of sound. The instrumentation for harmonium and piano was not unusual in France at the time; Lesueur, Gounod and Franck also wrote sacred works for piano and organ or harmonium. After the successful première, at the urging of his friends, Rossini prepared an orchestral version through which the Mass became known to a wider public; nevertheless in the long run it has not been able to prevail over the original instrumentation. Today however, the second piano part, which merely served to reinforce certain passages, is customarily integrated into the first piano part; this is also the case in the present edition.

The adjective „petite“ in the title refers only to the instrumentation; with a duration of over 80 minutes, the Mass is anything but small. Its fourteen parts contain the full Mass text; additionally Rossini inserted the hymn *O salutaris hostia*. The significance of the work lies in the richness of the musical rendering, in the *leggerezza* of the melodies and the playful lightness in the handling of the „scholarly“ style of church music. Exactly this may have been one of Rossini's intentions; he who was only slightly trained in counterpoint and who, among other things, received the advice from Beethoven to stay with the opera and to compose „many Barbieres“, put particular ambition in his last work into the treatment of traditional forms of sacred music. The *Christe* portion of the *Kyrie* to be performed a cappella is thus a reminiscence of the polyphonic vocal music of Palestrina's time. The brilliant double fugues in the *Gloria* and the *Credo* are inspired by the spirit of the *stile antico*. Rossini's study of Bach found its expression in the instrumental *Preludio religioso*. The depth of expression on the one hand and the ironical noncomformity on the other hand are the most peculiar features of this Mass. The tempo marking „Allegro Cristiano“ in the *Credo* and the skipping piano accompaniment of the choral fugues reveal the scoffer with a twinkle in his eye, while other parts such as the *Kyrie* and the *Agnus Dei* are overwhelmingly serious. Despite all the diversity, the consistency of the work remains preserved. The numerical order within the large sections, *Gloria* and *Credo*, is linked together through repetitions and spacious harmonic parallels such as the beginning of the *Gloria* and the *Sanctus*, for example, also attest to the formal perfection of the Mass.

Rossini accompanied his musical legacy with the following sentences, which are included in the original score: *„Dear God, here it is, the poor little Mass. Is this sacred music (musique sacrée) I have composed, or accursed music (sacrée musique)? I am made for the Opera buffa, as you well know. A bit of skill, a bit of heart, that is all. Be then praised and let me into paradise. G. Rossini. Passy 1863.“*

Christiane a Campo

PETITE MESSE SOLENNELLE

Erster Teil

1. Kyrie

Soli und Chor

Gioacchino Rossini (1792-1868)
Herausgegeben von Andreas Schenck

Andante maestoso (♪ = 108)

A
9
Soprani
Alti
sotto voce
SOLI e CORO
Tenori
sotto voce
Ky - ri - e, Ky - ri -
Bassi
sotto voce
Ky - ri - e, Ky - ri -
Ky - ri -
pp
cresc.
ppp
cresc. poco a poco
11
Soprani
sotto voce
Ky - ri - e e - le - i -
- e, Ky - ri - e e - le - i -
- e, Ky - ri - e e - le - i -
- e, Ky - ri - e e - le - i -
f

13
smorz.
- son, e - le - i - son, e - - - -
p
smorz.
- son, e - le - i - son, e - - - -
p
smorz.
- son, e - le - i - son, e - - - -
p
smorz.
- son, e - le - i - son, e - le - - -
p
smorz.
smorz.
15
- le - - - - - i - son,
- le - - - - - i - son,
- le - - - - - i - son,
- - - - - - i - son,
4
G
cresc.
p
cresc.

17
B
Ky - ri -
Ky - ri -
Ky - ri -
Ky - ri -
19
- e e - le - - i - son, Ky - - ri -
- e e - le - - i - son, Ky - ri -
- e e - le - - i - son, Ky - ri -
- e e - le - - i - son, Ky - ri -

21
- e e - le - i - son, Ky - ri -
- e e - le - i - son, Ky - ri -
- e e - le - i - son, Ky - ri -
- e e - le - i - son, Ky - ri -
pp
ppp
23
- e e - le - i - son, Ky - ri -
- e e - le - i - son, Ky - ri -
- e e - le - i - son, Ky - ri -
- e e - le - i - son, Ky - ri -
f
p

25
- e e - le - i - son, Ky - - ri-
- e e - le - i - son, Ky - - ri-
- e e - le - i - son, Ky - - ri-
- e e - le - i - son, Ky - - ri-
④
mf
p
27
f
pp
- e e - le - - - i - son, Ky - - ri-
- e e - le - - - i - son, Ky - - ri-
- e e - le - - - i - son, Ky - - ri-
- e e - le - - - i - son, Ky - - ri-

29
f
pp
pppp
- e e - le - - i - son, Ky - - ri -
- e e - le - - i - son, Ky - - ri -
- e e - le - - i - son, Ky - - ri -
- e e - le - - i - son, Ky - - ri -
f
pp
pppp
f
pp
ppp
31
- e, Ky - - ri - e e - le - i -
- e, Ky - - ri - e e - le - i -
- e, Ky - - ri - e e - le - i -
- e, Ky - - ri - e e - le - i -

33
- son.
- son.
- son.
- son.
morendo
morendo
36
Andantino moderato (𝅗𝅥 = 66)
tutto sotto voce e legato
sotto voce
Chri - ste
sotto voce
Chri - - ste, Chri - - ste e -
sotto voce
Chri - - ste e - le - - - -
sotto voce
Chri - ste, Chri - - ste e le - - - i - son,
40
e - le - - - - - - - - - - -
- le - - i - son, Chri - - ste e -
- - - - - - i - son,
Chri - ste e - le - - - - - - i - son,

43
- - - i - - son,
Chri - - - ste e -
- le - - - - - - - i - son,
Chri - - - ste e - - le - - - - - - - i - - -
Chri - - - ste e - - - - -
46
- le - - - - - - i - son,
Chri - ste e -
Chri - - ste e - - - - le - i - son,
Chri - ste e -
- son,
Chri - ste e - le - - i - son,
e -
- le - i - son,
Chri - ste e - le - - - i - son,
50
- le - i - son,
e - le - - - i - son, e - - - - -
- le - - i - son,
e - - - - le - - - i - son,
- le - - - i - son, e - - - - le - - - i - son,
e - - - le - - - i - son,
e - le - i -
54
Più lento
- - le - i - son,
e - - - le - - - i - son.
Chri - - - ste
e - - - le - - - i - son.
Chri - - - ste
e - - - le - - - i - son.
- son, e - le - - - - - - - i - son.

C
58
Tempo I (♪= 108)
①
ppp
①
ppp
stacc.
60
sotto voce
Ky - ri - e, Ky - ri -
sotto voce
Ky - ri - e, Ky - ri -
sotto voce
Ky - ri -
⓪
⓪
cresc.
cresc. poco a poco

62
sotto voce
Ky - ri - e e - le - i -
- e, Ky - ri - e e - le - i -
- e. Ky - ri - e e - le - i -
- e, Ky - ri - e e - le - i -
f
④
64
smorz.
- son, e - le - i - son, e -
- son, e - le - i - son, e -
- son, e - le - i - son, e -
- son, e - le - i - son, e - le -
p

66
D
pp
pppp
-le - - - - - i - - son, Ky - ri -
-le - - - - - i - - son, Ky - ri -
-le - - - - - i - - son, Ky - ri -
- - - - - - i - - son, Ky - ri -
p
ppp
68
f
p
-e e-le - - i-son, Ky - - ri -
-e e-le - - i - son, Ky - ri -
-e e-le - - i - son, Ky - ri -
-e e-le - - i - son, Ky - ri -

70
pppp
- e e - le - i - son, Ky - ri -
- e e - le - i - son, Ky - ri -
- e e - le - i - son, Ky - ri -
- e e - le - i - son, Ky - ri -
p
pppp
72
f
p
- e e - le - i - son, Ky - ri -
- e e - le - i - son, Ky - ri -
- e e - le - i - son, Ky - ri -
- e e - le - i - son, Ky - ri -

74
- e e - le - i - son, e - le - i -
- e e - le - i - son, e - le - i -
- e e - le - i - son, e - le - i -
- e e - le - i - son, e - le - i -
pp
ppp
76
- son, e - le - i - son, e - le - - i -
- son, e - le - i - son, e - le - i -
- son, e - le - i - son, e - le - i -
- son, e - le - i - son, e - le - i -
p
f

78
- son, e - le - i - son, e - le - i -
- son, e - le - i - son, e - le - i -
- son, e - le - i - son, e - le - i -
- son, e - le - i - son, e - le - i -
p ppp
80
- son, e - le - i - son, Ky - - ri -
- son. e - le - i - son, Ky - - ri -
- son, e - le - i - son, Ky - - ri -
- son, e - le - i - son, Ky - - ri -
p f p mf p
f p

82
f
pp
e e-le - - i - son, Ky - - ri-
mf
pppp
84
e e-le - - i - son, Ky - - ri-
ppp
4

86
- e, Ky - - ri - e e - le - i -
- e, Ky - - ri - e e - le - i -
- e, Ky - - ri - e e - le - i -
- e, Ky - - ri - e e - le - i -
88
- son.
- son.
- son.
- son.
morendo
morendo

2. Gloria

Soli und Chor

ff
Glo - - ri- a,
Glo - - ri- a
F
Andantino mosso (𝅗𝅥 = 58)
ppp
rall. . . . .
G
(𝅗𝅥 = 58) in tempo
Basso solo
Et in ter - ra pax ho - mi-ni-bus bo - næ vo - lun - ta - -
pppp

33
Soprano solo
Lau - da - mus te
Alto solo
Lau - da - mus
Tenore solo
Lau - da - mus
- tis.
Lau - - - da - mus
①
ppp
41
Be - ne - di - ci - mus te
te
Be - ne - di - ci - mus te
te
Be - ne - di - ci - mus te
te
Be - ne - di - ci - mus te
ppp

48
A - do - ra - mus te,
A - do - ra - mus te,
A - do - ra - mus te, A - do - ra - mus
A - - do - ra - mus te,
ppp
55
A - do - ra - mus te, A - - do - ra - mus
A - - do - ra - mus te,
te, A - - do - ra - - - - mus
A - do - ra - mus te, A - - do - ra - - - mus
ppp

61
te
Glo - ri - fi - ca - mus te,
Glo - ri - fi - ca- - - - - - mus te,
te
Glo - ri - fi-
te
Glo - ri - fi - ca - - - mus te,
④
③
66
Glo - ri - fi - ca- - - - - mus te,
Glo - ri - fi - ca - mus te,
- ca- - - - - - mus te,
Tutti
Glo - - ri - fi - ca - mus te, A - do - ra - mus
③

71
Tutti
A - do - ra - mus
Tutti
A - do - ra - mus te,
Tutti
A - do - ra - mus te,
te,
77
sotto voce
te, Glo - ri - fi - ca - mus te.
sotto voce
Glo - ri - fi - ca - mus te.
sotto voce
Glo - ri - fi - ca - mus te.
sotto voce
Glo - ri - fi - ca - mus te.
pppp

3. Gratias

Soli (Alt, Tenor, Baß)

31
Alto solo
A.
Gra - ti-as a - gi-mus ti - - bi
B.
glo - ri-am tu- - - am.Gra-ti-as a-gi-mus a-gi-mus ti - bi
37
A.
prop - ter ma - gnam glo - ri-am, glo - ri-am tu- - - am.Gra-ti-as
Tenore solo
T.
Gra - ti-as
B.
prop-ter ma-gnam glo-ri-am, glo-ri-am tu- - - am. Gra-ti-
43
A.
a - gi-mus, a - gi-mus ti - bi prop - ter ma - gnam
T.
a - gi-mus ti - - bi prop - ter ma - gnam
B.
- as a - gi - mus ti - bi, ti- - - bi prop-ter ma-gnam

48
A.
glo-ri-am, glo-ri-am tu- - - -am,
T.
glo - ri-am, glo - ri-am, glo-ri-am tu - am, prop - ter
B.
glo - ri-am, glo - ri-am tu- - - -am, prop - ter ma-gnam,
53
ff
Glo - ri - am tu- - -
ma-gnam, prop - ter ma-gnam, Glo - ri - am tu- - -
prop - ter ma-gnam, Glo - ri - am tu- - -
smorz.
58
- - - am.
- - - am.
- - - am.
pppp

64
I
ppp
A.
Gra - ti - as a - gi - mus ti - - -
T.
Gra - ti - as a - gi - mus, a - gi - mus
B.
Gra - ti - as a - gi - mus, a - gi - mus
pp
ppp
70
A.
- bi Prop - ter ma - gnam glo - ri - am, glo - ri - am
T.
ti - bi Prop - ter ma - gnam glo - ri - am, glo - ri - am
B.
ti - bi Prop - ter ma - gnam glo - ri - am, glo - ri - am
75
A.
tu - - - am, Prop - ter ma -
T.
tu - - - am, Prop - ter ma - gnam, ma -
B.
tu - - - am, Prop - ter ma - gnam glo - ri - am tu -
cresc.

80
A.
T.
B.
f
pp
-gnam, Prop - ter ma - gnam glo - ri - am_tu - am,
-gnam, Prop - ter ma - gnam glo - ri - am tu - am,
- am,___ Prop - ter__ ma - gnam glo - ri - am tu - am, Prop - ter__
smorz.
85
cresc.
Prop - ter___ ma - gnam, Prop - ter ma -
Prop - ter___ ma - gnam,__ ma - gnam, Prop - ter ma -
___ ma - gnam__Glo - ri - am tu - am,__ Prop - ter__ ma -
90
ppp
mf
-gnam glo - ri - am_tu - am, glo - ri - am, glo - ri - am tu - am,
-gnam glo - ri - am tu - am, Glo-ri - am,__
-gnam__ glo - ri - am_tu - am, Glo-ri - am,__

95
A.
T.
B.
sotto voce
Glo - - ri - -
gloriam tu - - am,
sotto voce
Glo - - ri - -
gloriam tu - - am,
sotto voce
Glo - - ri - -
mf
ppp
100
-am
tu - - - - - am.
-am
tu - - - - - am.
-am
tu - - - - - am.
105
pppp
110
pppp
morendo

4. Domine Deus

Tenor solo

25
-tens Do-mi - ne fi - li u - - - ni-
29
-ge - ni-te Je - - - su, Je - - - su Chri - -
33
-ste, Je - su Chri - ste, Je - su
37
Chri - ste, Do-mi - ne De - - us rex cœ-
41
-le-stis De- - -us Pa-ter om-ni- - - po-

45
pp
cresc.
tens, Do - mi - ne fi - li u - ni -
3
pp
49
rinf.
f
ge - ni - te, u - ni - ge - ni - te Je - su Chri -
mf
f
53
L
ste.
ff
57
ff
61
M
Do - mi - ne De - us
ppp
65
A - gnus De - i

69
Fi - li - us Pa - - - tris,
73
Fi - li - us Pa - - - tris,
77
Do - mi-ne De - us A - gnus De - i,
81
A - gnus De - i Fi - li - us Pa - tris,
pppp
85
Fi - li - us Pa - - - tris. Do - mi - ne

89
De - us Rex cœ - le - - stis De - - - - us
pp
pp
93
Pa - ter om - - ni - - po - tens Do - mi - - ne
ff
pp
97
Fi - li u - - - ni - ge - ni - te Je - - - su,
pp
pp
101
Je - - - su Chri - - - ste, Je - su
ff
pp
105
Chri - ste, Je - su Chri - ste, Do - mi - ne
N
ff
sf

109
De - - us Rex cœ - le - stis De - - us
sf
sf
ff
sf
113
Pa - ter om - ni - - po - tens Do - mi - ne
sf
sf
ppp
117
Fi - li u - ni - ge - ni - te, u - ni -
cresc.
rinf.
mf
121
- ge - - ni-te Je - su Chri - - ste. Do - mi - ne
f
f
pp
125
O
De - us A - - gnus De - i
cresc.
f

128
f
Fi - - li - - us Pa - - - tris, Fi - - li - - us
ff
131
Pa- - - - - - - - - - tris, Fi - - li - us
smorz.
pp
134
Pa- - - - - - tris, Do- - mi - ne
pp
137
De - us A - - - gnus De - i
cresc.
f
140
f
Fi - - li - - us Pa- - - tris, Fi - - li - - us
ff

143
Pa- tris, Fi- li- us
smorz.
pp
146
Pa- tris. Fi- li- us Pa- tris, Fi- li- us
ff
ff
sf
sf
150
Pa- tris.
sf
sf
ff
153
p
156
tr
f
p
pp
pp
160
ppp
ff

5. Qui tollis

Soli (Sopran, Alt)

13
S.
- ca - - ta, pec-ca - - - ta mun - - di
A.
- ca - - ta, pec-ca - - - ta mun - - di
16
S.
mi - se-re - re no - - bis, mi - se-re - re
A.
mi - se-re - re no - - bis, mi - se-re - re
Harmonium
pp
pp
19
S.
no - - bis. Qui tol - lis pec - ca - - ta
A.
no - - bis. Qui
ppp

22
cresc.
pec - ca -
cresc.
tol - lis pec - ca - - - ta, pec - ca - ta
ppp
pp
cresc.
cresc.
25
f
pp
f
- - ta, pec - ca - - - ta mun - di mi - se-
mun - di, pec - ca - - - ta mun - di
mf
28
pp
f
- re - - - re no - - bis, mi - se - re - - - re
mi - se-re - re no - - bis, mi - se-re - re
④
④

31
pp
no - - bis, mi - se - - re - re
pp
no - - bis, mi - - se - - re - - re
③
ppp
③
pp
34
ppp
no - - - bis.
ppp
no - - - bis.
③④
③④
G
ff
G
ppp
mf
ff
Q
37
(♩=84)
Qui tol - - lis pec - ca - - ta pec-
ppp
pp

40
-ca- - -ta mun- - -di su-sci- - -pe
pp
43
de-pre-ca-ti-o-nem no- - -stram
Qui
46
tol- - -lis pec-ca- - -ta pec-ca- - -ta
ppp

49
mun- - - di su - sci - - pe de - pre - ca - ti - o - nem no - -
pp
53
R
ppp
de - - pre - ca - - - ti - o - - - nem no - stram, de - - pre-
- stram, de - - pre - ca - - - ti - o - - - nem no - stram, de - - pre-
56
rall.
f
a tempo
- ca - - - ti - o - - nem no - - - stram. Qui se - - - des ad
- ca - - - ti - o - - nem no - - - stram. Qui se - - - des ad
col canto
ff

59
dex - te - ram, ad dex - - - te - - ram Pa - - tris
dex - te - ram, ad dex - - - te - ram Pa - - tris
62
mi - - se - re - - re no - - - bis, mi - - se - re - - re
mi - - se - re - - re no - - - bis, mi - - se - re - - re
65
no - - - bis. Qui se - des ad dex - - te - ram
no - - - bis. Qui

68
cresc.
Qui se-
se - des ad dex - te-ram, Qui se - des,
cresc.
cresc.
71
f
pp
f
- des ad dex - te - ram Pa - tris, mi - se-
se - des ad dex - te - ram Pa - tris,
mf
pp
74
pp
f
- re - re no - bis, mi - se - re - re
mi - se-re - re no - bis, mi - se-re - re
4

77
pp
no - - bis, mi - - se - - - re - - - re
no - - bis, mi - - se - - re - - re
pp
ppp
80
ppp
no - - - - bis.
S
(♩=80)
f
Qui se - - - des, Qui
Qui se - - - des, Qui
ff
83
se - - - des ad dex - - te - ram Pa - - - tris, Qui
se - - - des ad dex - - te - ram Pa - - - tris, Qui

86
se - - des, Qui se - - des ad dex - te - ram Pa - -
se - - des, Qui se - - des ad dex - te - ram Pa - -
89
-tris mi - se - re - re mi - - se -
-tris mi - se - re - re, mi - - se-
pp
pp
pp
92
cresc.
f
- - re - - - re no - bis, mi - - se - re - - - re
cresc.
- re - - re, mi - - se - re - - re, mi - - se - re - - re
pp cresc.
f
cresc.
f

95
no - - bis, mi - se - re - re no - - bis, mi - se -
no - - bis, mi - se - re - re no - - bis,
98
- re - re, mi - - se - - re - - re
mi - se - re - re, mi - - se - re - - re, mi - - se-
101
no - bis, mi - - se - re - - re no - - bis, mi - se -
- re - - re, mi - - se - re - - re no - - bis, mi - se -
cresc.
ff
pp
ppp
f

104
pp
-re - re no - - bis, mi - se-re - re no- - - - -
pp
-re - re no - - bis, mi - se-re - re no- - - - - -
ppp
pp
107
a piacere
f
a tempo
- bis, mi - se-re-re, mi - se - re- - re no- - - bis.
f
- bis, mi - se-re-re, mi - se - re- - re no- - - bis.
col canto
pppp
col canto
ppp
110

6. Quoniam tu solus sanctus

Baß solo

T Basso solo
Quo - ni - am tu so - lus sanc - tus,
pp
Quo - ni - am tu so - lus sanc - tus Tu
so - lus Do - mi-nus, tu so - lus Do - mi-nus Tu
simile stacc.
so - lus al - tis - si-mus Je - su Chri - ste,
ff
ff
p
Je - su, Je - su Chri - ste, Tu
mf
cresc.
ff
ff
f

so - lus, Tu so - lus al - tis - si - mus, al -
- tis - si - mus Je - su Chri - ste, Tu so - lus al -
- tis - si - mus Je - su, Je - su Chri -
U
- ste.
Tu so - lus

68
sanc - tus Tu so - lus Do - mi-nus Tu so - lus al -
simile stacc.
tr
72
- tis - si-mus, tu so - lus al - tis - si - mus Je - su
cresc.
ff
76
V
Chri-ste.
Quo - ni-am tu so - lus, tu
f
mf
ppp
81
so - lus sanc - tus Tu so - lus Do - mi - nus Tu so - lus al -
86
- tis - si - mus Je - su Chri - ste, Tu so - lus sanc - tus Tu
f
pp
ppp

91
so - lus Do - mi-nus Tu so - lus al - tis - si-mus Je - su
cresc.
96
W
Chri - - ste, Je-su Chri - - ste. Tu
f
ff
pp
100
so - - - lus, Tu so - - - lus
103
al - - tis- - - si - mus Je - - - su
106
Chri- - - - - - ste, Tu
ppp
f
f
f
mf

110
so - - - lus, tu so - - - lus al - tis - si-mus, Al -
pp f f
114
- tis - si - mus Je - - su Chri - - ste, Tu
ff ff
117
so - - lus al - tis - - si-mus Je - su, Je - su
pp
120
tr
Chri - - - - ste.
f ff ff f
123
pp ff f pp

127
Tu so - lus sanc - - tus Tu so - lus
pp
simile stacc.
tr
131
Do - mi-nus Tu so - lus al - tis - - si-mus, Tu so - - lus al -
cresc.
135
- tis - - si - - mus Je - - - su Chri-ste.
X
ff
mf
139
Quo - - ni-am Tu so - - lus, tu so - - lus
ppp
143
sanc - - tus Tu so - - lus Do - mi - nus Tu so - - lus al -
cresc.

147
-tis- - -si- - -mus Je- - -su Chri- - - -ste, Tu so- - -lus
f pp pppp
151
sanc- -tus Tu so- - -lus Do- -mi-nus Tu so- - -lus al-
cresc.
155
-tis- - -si-mus Je- - -su Chri- - -ste, Je-su Chri- - -
rinf. f ff
Y
159
-ste. Tu so- - -lus,
pp stacc.
162
Tu so- - -lus Al- -

165
-tis- -si-mus Je- -su Chri- - - - - - - -
ppp
169
-ste, Tu so- - -lus, tu so- - -lus Al- -
f f f pp
173
-tis-si-mus, Al-tis-si-mus Je- -su Chri- -
f f ff
177
-ste, Tu so- - -lus al-tis- si-mus Je-su, Je-su
ff ff fp
181
tr
Chri- - - -ste. Tu so- - -lus Je- -su
f f

184
Chri - - - - - ste, Tu so - - - lus Je - - - su
ff
187
Je - - - - - su Chri - - - ste.
Z
8
fff
ff
191
f
ff
195
f
ff
f
200
ff
pp
205
Subito
Cum Sancto Spiritu

7. Cum sancto spiritu

Soli und Chor

17
ff
A - - - -men, A - - - -men.
A - - - -men, A - - - -men.
A - - - -men, A - - - -men.
A - - - -men, A - - - -men.
21
3

A
26
Allegro a capella
Cum Sanc-to Spi-ri-tu in Glo-ri-a De-i Pa-tris A-
A- men, A-
mf
stacc.
30
men, A- men, A-
men, Cum Sanc-to

34
-men, A - - - - - - men, A - - - - -
Spi - ri-tu in Glo - ri - a De - i Pa - tris A - - - - men,
38
- - - - - - men, A - - - - -
A - - - - - men, A -
Tenori
Cum Sanc - to Spi - ri-tu in

42
men, A-
men, A-
Glo - ri- a De - i Pa - tris A- - men,
46
B
men, A- - men, A-
men, A-
men, A-
Bassi
Cum Sanc - to Spi - ri - tu in Glo - ri - a De - i

50
men, A-
men, A-
Pa-tris A- men, A-
③
③
54
men. A- men. A-
men, A- men. A-
men, A- men, A- men. A-
men, A- men, A-
G
ff
ff

58
-men, A- - - - men, A- - - - -
- - men, A- - - men, A- - - - -
-men, A-men, A- - men, A- - - -
-men, A- - - men, A- - - -
62
-men, A- - - - - - - - - -
- - men, A- - - - - - - - -
-men, A- - - - - - - -
-men, A-men, A- - - - - - -

66
- men, A-
- men, A-
- men, A-
- men, A - men, A-
70
- men, A - men, A-
- men, A - men, A-
- men, A - men, A - men,
- men, A - men, A - men, A-
ff

74
-men, A- men, A-
men, A-
A- men, A- men, A-
78

82
C
men,
men, Cum Sanc - to Spi - ri - tu in
men, A -
men,
mf
mf
86
A - men, A -
Glo - ri - a De - i Pa - tris A - men, A -
men, A -

90
men,
men, A - men, A -
- men, Cum Sanc - to Spi - ri - tu in Glo - ri - a De - i
94
A -
- men, A - - men, A -
Pa - tris A - - men, A -
①
①

98
-men, A- - - - - - - - -
-men, A- - - - - - - - - men, A-
-men, A- - -men, A- - - - - - - -
Cum Sanc-to Spi-ri-tu in Glo-ri-a De-i Pa-tris A-
③
③
102
- - - - - - - -men, Cum Sanc-to
- - - - - - - - - - - men,
- - - - - - - - - - - - men, A- -
-men, A- - - - - - men, A-

106
Spi - ri - tu in Glo - ri - a De - i Pa - tris A - - - men,
A - - - - - - men, A - - - - -
- - - - - - - - men, A - - - - - -
- - men, A - - - - - - - - - - - -
110
A - - - - - - - - - men, A - - - -
- - - - - - - - - men, A - - - - - - -
- - - - - - - - men, A - - - -
- - - - - - - - - men, A - men, A -

114
-men, A- - - - - - - - men, A- - - -
-men, A- - - - - - - - - men, A- - - -
-men. A- - - - - - - - men. A- - - -
-men. A- - - - - - - - men. A - men, A-
ff
f
118
-men, A- - - - - - - men, A- - - - -
-men, A- - - - - - - - men, A- - - -
-men, A- - - - - - - men, A- - - -
-men, A- - - - - - - - men, A - men, A- - -
ff

122
men, A -
men, A -
men, A -
men, A - men, A -
126
D
men, A - men, A -
men,
A -
men, A - men, A -
men, A -
f

130
smorzando
smorzando
smorzando
smorzando
smorzando
smorzando
134
- men,
A - - - - - men,
A - - - - -
- men,
A - - - - - men,
A - - - - -
- men,
A - - - - - men,
A - - - - -
- men,
A - - - - - men,
A - - - - -
pppp
pppp

138
men,
men,
A
men,
A
men,
142
men,
A
men,
A
men,
A
men,
A
men,
A
men,
men,
A

146
A
④
④
150

154
158
cresc.
men,
men, A -
men, A -
③

162
E
Cum Sanc - to Spi - ri - tu in Glo - ri - a De - i Pa - tris A -
- men. A - - - - - - men,
- men. A - - - - - - - - men, A - - -
- men.
stacc.
166
- men. A - - - men. A - - - -
Cum Sanc-to Spi - ri - tu in Glo - ri - a De - i Pa - tris A -
- men. A - - - - - - men,
A - - - - - - - men, A - - -

170
-men, A- - - - - - - - - - men, A- - - -
-men, A- - - - - - - - - men.
Cum Sanc-to Spi - ri-tu in Glo-ri-a De-i Pa-tris A- -
-men, A- - - - - - - - - men.
174
-men. A- - - - - - - - -
A- - - - - - - - - - men, A- - -
-men, A- - - - - - - - - - - -
Cum Sanc-to Spi - ri-tu in Glo-ri-a De-i Pa-tris A- -

178
-men, A-men A-
-men, A-
-men, A-
-men, A-
ff
ff
182
-men, A-men, A-
men, A-
-men, A-
men, A-
-men, A-
men, A-
-men, A-
men, A-

186
-men, A- - - - men, A- - - - men, A- - - - men, A- - - -
-men, A- - - - men, A- - - - men, A- - - - men, A- - - -
-men, A- - - - men, A- - - - men, A- - - - men, A- - - -
-men, A- - - - men, A- - - - men, A- - - - men, A- - - -
190
F
ff
-men, A- - - - - - - - men, A- - - - - - - -
-men, A- - - - - - - - men, A- - - - - - - -
-men, A- - - - men, A- - - -
-men, A- - - - - - - - men, A- - - - - - - -

194
-men, A - - - - - - - -men,
-men, A - - - - - - - -men, A - - - - men,
-men, A - - -men, A - - - - - -
-men, A - - - - - - - - -men, A - - - - - -
198
A - - - men, A - - - men, fff A - - -
A - - men, A - - men, A - - men, A - men, fff A - - -
- - - - - - - - - - - men, fff A - - -
- - - - - - - - - - - men, fff A - - -
sim.
fff
fff

203
G
- men, A- - - - - - - men.
- men, A- - - - - - - men.
- men, A- - - - - - - men.
- men, A- - - - - - - men.
ff
ff
207

212
Glo - ri - a in ex - cel - sis,
Glo - ri - a in ex - cel - sis,
Glo - ri - a in ex - cel - sis,
Glo - ri - a in ex - cel - sis,
ff
ff
217

222
Animando un poco
f
ff
in ex- cel - sis De - - o A - - men,
in ex- cel - sis De - - o A - - - - -
in ex- cel - sis De - - o A - - - - - - -
in ex- cel - sis De - - o A - - - - -
Animando un poco
227
A - men, A - men,
- men, A - - men, A - - - -
-men, A - - - - - - - men, A- - - - - - -
-men, A - - - - - men, A - - - -
sim.

231
A - men, A -
men, A - men, A -
men, A - men, A -
men, A - men, A -
235
men, A -
men, A -
men, A -
men, A -
fff
fff

239
men, A - men, A - men, A - men,
men, A - men, A -
men, A - men,
men, A - men, A -
243
A - men, A -
men, A -
A - men, A -
men,

247
men,
men,
men,
A
men,
252
A
men,
ff
A
ff
men,
ff
A
A
men,
A
men,
A
men,
A
men,
A
men,
A
men,
A
men,
A
fff
fff
fff

257
men.
men.
men.
men.
ff
8
ff
262
ff
fff
8
ff
fff

Zweiter Teil

8. Credo

Soli und Chor

8
ff
pp
Cre - - - do in u - num De - um,
Alti
Cre - - - do
Cre - - - do in u - num De - um,
Bassi
Cre - - - do
fff
pp
13
Cre - - - do in u - num De - um, Cre - - -
in u - num De - um, Cre - - -
Cre - - - do in u - num De - um, Cre - - -
in u - num De - um, Cre - - -
f

18
ppp
-do Pa- - - trem o-mni-po -ten- - -
-do Pa- - - trem o-mni-po -ten- - -
-do Pa- - - trem o-mni-po -ten- - -
-do Pa- - - trem o-mni-po -ten- - -
pp
pp
pp
22
-tem
Alto solo
-tem Fac- to -rem coe -li et
-tem
Bassi solo
-tem Fac- to -rem coe- li et ter - rae. Fac- to -rem coe -li et

26
Soprano solo
Fac- to - rem coe - li et ter - rae vi - si - bi - li - um
ter - rae, Fac- to - rem coe - li et ter - rae vi - si - bi - li - um
Tenore solo
vi - si - bi - li - um
ter - rae, Fac- to - rem coe - li et ter - rae vi - si - bi - li - um
p
30
om - ni - um et in - vi - si - bi - li - um.
om - ni - um et in - vi - si - bi - li - um.
om - ni - um et in - vi - si - bi - li - um.
om - ni - um et in - vi - si - bi - li - um.
f

H
33
Tutti
Cre - - - do, Cre - - - -
- do in u - num De - um, Cre - - do in
Tutti
Cre - - - do, Cre - - - -
- do
in
Tutti
Cre - - - do, Cre - - - -
- do in u - num De - um, Cre - - do in
Tutti
Cre - - - do, Cre - - - -
- do
in
ff
pp
36

41
ppp
u - num De - um, Cre - - - do Et in
ppp
u - num De - um, Cre - - - do Et in
ppp
u - num De - um, Cre - - - do Et in
ppp
u - num De - um, Cre - - - do Et in
f
f
pp
45
u - num Do - mi - num Je - - - sum Chri - stum
u - num Do - mi - num Je - - - sum Chri - stum
u - num Do - mi - num Je - - - sum Chri - stum
u - num Do - mi - num Je - - - sum Chri - stum
pp

49
Soprano solo
U - - ni - - ge - - ni-tum
Alto solo
Fi - - li - um De - - i U - - ni - - ge - - ni-tum
53
an - - te om - - ni - a
Et ex pa - tre na - - tum an - - te om - - ni - a
Tenore solo
Et ex pa - tre na - - tum an - - te om - - ni - a
Basso solo
Et ex pa - tre na - - tum an - - te om - - ni - a

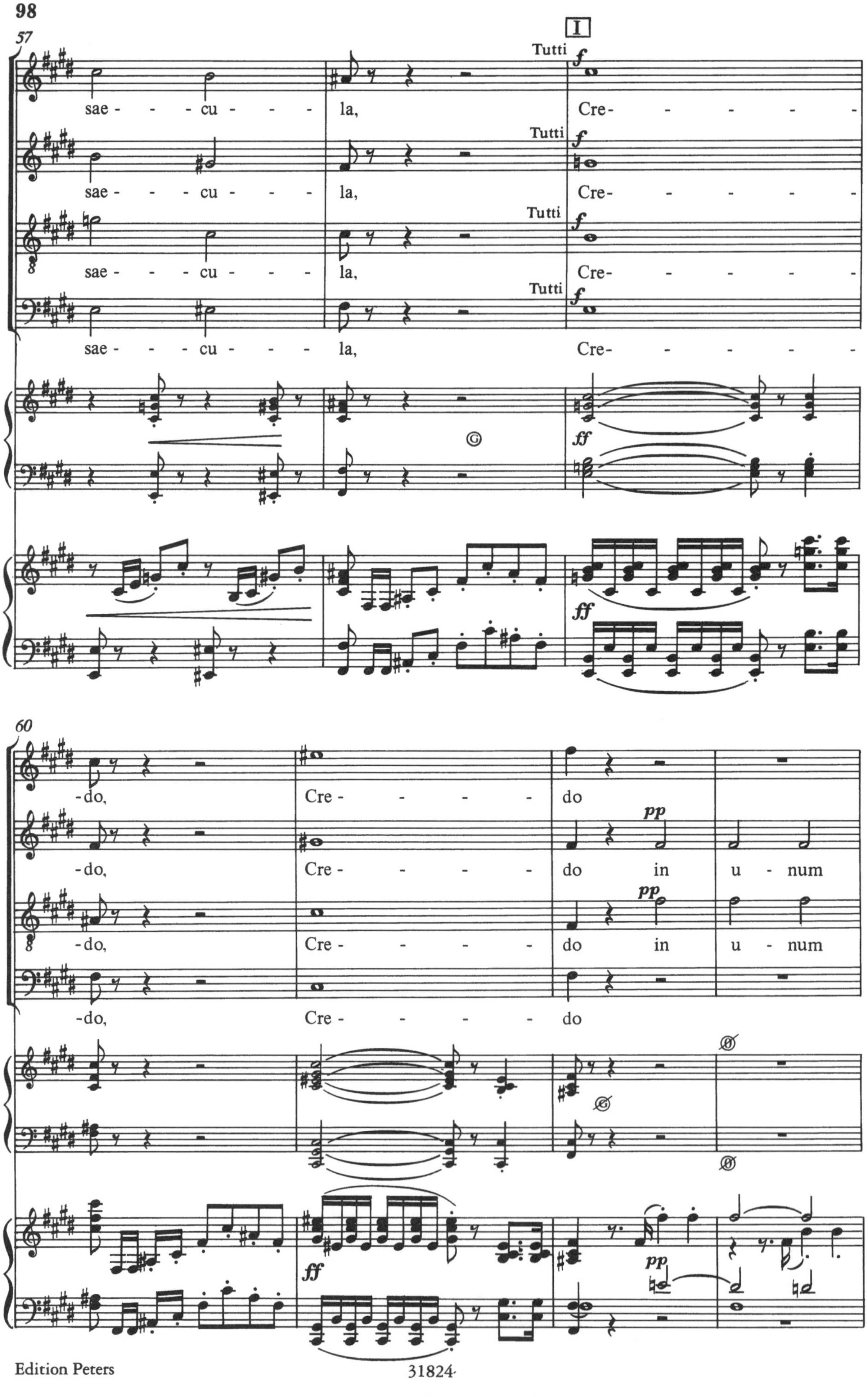
57
I
Tutti
sae - - - cu - - - la, Cre- - - - - -
Tutti
sae - - - cu - - - la, Cre- - - - - -
Tutti
sae - - - cu - - - la, Cre- - - - - -
Tutti
sae - - - cu - - - la, Cre- - - - - -
ff
ff
60
-do, Cre - - - - - do
-do, Cre - - - - - do in u - num
-do, Cre - - - - - do in u - num
-do, Cre - - - - - do
pp
pp
ff
pp

64
in u - num De - um,
De - um, Cre - - do in u - num De - um,
De - um, Cre - - do in u - num De - um,
in u - num De - um,
pp
69
ppp
Cre - - - - - do De - um de De - o
ppp
Cre - - - - - do De - um de De - o
ppp
Cre - - - - - do De - um de De - o
ppp
Cre - - - - - do De - um de De - o
f
pp
f
pp

73
lu - men de lu - mi-ne
lu - men de lu - mi-ne
Tenore solo
lu - men de lu - mi-ne De - - um ve - - rum
lu - men de lu - mi-ne
77
Soprano solo
Ge - ni - tum non fac - - tum
Alto solo
de De - o ve - - ro.
Ge - ni - tum non fac - - tum
Basso solo
de De - o ve - - ro Ge - ni - tum non fac - - tum

81
con - sub-stan - ti - a - lem Pa - - - -
con - sub-stan - ti - a - lem Pa - - - -
con - sub-stan - ti - a - lem Pa - - - -
con - sub-stan - ti - a - lem Pa - - - -
84
K
Tutti
- tri fac - - ta
Tutti
- tri fac - ta, fac - - - - - ta
Tutti
- tri per quem om - ni - a fac - - - - ta
Tutti
- tri per quem om - ni - a fac - ta fac - - - - ta

88
sunt
sunt
prop - ter nos
sunt
qui prop - - ter nos
sunt qui prop - ter, prop - - ter nos ho - - mi - nes,
f
91
nos ho - mi - nes
ho - - - - mi - nes
ho - - - - mi - nes
et prop - ter
ho - - - - mi - nes et prop - ter no - - - stram sa -
ff
ff

94
sa - lu - - tem de-
no - stram sa - lu - - - - - - tem de-
no - - stram sa - lu - - - - - - tem de-
- lu - - tem, sa - lu - - - - - - tem de-
ff
G
97
- scen - dit de coe - lis, de- scen - dit de

100
coe - lis, de- scen - dit de coe - - - -
coe - lis, de- scen - dit de coe - - - -
coe - lis, de- scen - dit de coe - - - -
coe - lis, de- scen - dit de coe - - - -
103
L
f
lis, cre - - - -
lis, cre - - - -
lis, cre - - - -
lis, cre - - - -
ff
ff

106
Soprano solo
sotto voce
-do, cre - - - do Et
Alto solo
sotto voce
-do, cre - - - do Et in - car -
Tenore solo
sotto voce
-do, cre - - - do Et in - car -
-do, cre - - - do
ten.
ff
pp
110
in - car-na - tus est de
-na- - - tus est de Spi - ri - tu Sanc - to
-na- - - tus est de Spi - ri - tu Sanc - to
Basso solo
sotto voce
in - car-na - tus est de
pp
ten.

115
Spi - ri - tu Sanc - to ex Ma-
Spi - ri - tu Sanc - to ex Ma - ri - a, ex Ma -
Spi - ri - tu Sanc - to ex Ma - ri - a, ex Ma -
Spi - ri - tu Sanc - to ex Ma-
ten.
119
- ri - a Vir - gi-ne et ho - mo
- ri - a Vir - gi-ne et ho - mo
- ri - a Vir - gi-ne
- ri - a Vir - gi-ne
Tutti ff
f
ff

123
fac - - tus est.
fac - - tus est.
Tutti ff
et ho - - - mo fac - - - tus
Tutti ff
et ho - - - mo fac - - - tus
128
est.
est.
8
f
pp
8
f
pp
132
8
f
pp
8
f
pp

9. Crucifixus

Sopran solo

13
-la - to pas - sus, pas - sus et se-pul - tus
17
est, pas - sus, pas - sus et se-pul - tus
pp f pp
21
M
est, cru - ci - fi - xus, cru - ci-
pp

25
-fi - xus, cru - ci - fi - xus, cru - ci -
pp
29
f
-fi - xus e - ti-am pro no - bis, e - ti-am pro no - bis sub
f
f
34
Pon - ti-o Pi - la - to; sub Pon -ti-o Pi - la - to pas - sus,—
pp

39
pas - sus et se-pul - tus est, pas - sus,
f
pp
43
pas - - sus et se-pul - tus est, et se-pul-tus
pp
ppp
47
est, et se-pul-tus est.
morendo

10. Et resurrexit

Soli und Chor

9
- e
se - - cun - -
fff
fff
14
- dum scrip - tu - - - - - - ras,
f

18
f
Cre - - - - do, Cre - - - -
f
Cre - - - - do, Cre - - - -
f
Cre - - - - do, Cre - - - -
f
Cre - - - - do, Cre - - - -
ff
ff
21
- do
- do
- do
- do

25
ff
ff
29
N
CORO
pp
Et a - scen - dit, a - scen - dit in
Et a - scen - dit, a - scen - dit in
Et a - scen - dit, a - scen - dit in
Et a - scen - dit, a - scen - dit in
pp
pp

33
coe - lum,
Alto solo
coe - lum, A - scen - dit in
coe - lum,
Basso solo
coe - lum, Et a - - scen - - dit, a - scen - dit in
37
Soprano solo
se - - - det ad dex - te-ram, se - - - det ad
coe - - lum se - - - det ad dex - te-ram, se - - - det ad
Tenore solo
se - det ad
coe - - lum se - - det ad dex - te-ram, se - - det ad

41
dex - te - ram pa - tris
dex - te - ram pa - tris
dex - te - ram pa - tris
Tutti
dex - te - ram pa - tris Et
cresc.
Ⓐ ff
ff
44
Tutti
Et i - terum ven - tu - rus est cum
Tutti
Et i - terum ven - tu - rus est cum
Tutti
Et i - terum ven - tu - rus est cum
i - terum ven - tu - rus est cum

47
glo - ri - a ju - di -
glo - ri - a ju - di -
glo - ri - a ju - di -
glo - ri - a ju - di - ca - re

50
- ca - re vi - vos et mor - tu -
- ca - re vi - vos et mor - tu -
- ca - re vi - vos et mor - tu -
vi - vos, vi - vos et mor - tu -

53
- os
cu - jus
re - - gni non
- os
cu - jus
re - - gni non
- os
cu - jus
re - - gni non
- os cu - jus re - - - gni,
re - - gni non
56
e - - - rit
fi - - - - - -
nis
e - - - rit
fi - - - - - -
nis
e - - - rit
fi - - - - - -
nis
e - - - rit
fi - - - - - -
nis et in
f

59
Do - - mi -
Sanc - tum Do - - - - - mi -
Spi - ri - tum Sanc - tum Do - - - - - mi -
Spi - - - ri - tum Sanc - tum Do - - - - - mi -
ff
ff
62
num
- num vi - vi - fi -
- num et vi - vi - - fi -
- num et vi - vi - fi - can - - - tem, vi - vi - fi -
f

65
vi - vi - fi-can - - -tem
-can - - - - - -tem
-can - - - - - -tem Pa - - tre
-can - - - - - -tem qui ex Pa - tre Fi - li -
ff
f
68
O
pro - ce - - -dit
Fi - li- o - que pro - ce - - - - - dit
Fi - li - o - que pro - ce - - - - - dit
- o - - que pro - ce - - - - - dit
ff
ten. pp
pp

71
sotto voce
qui cum Pa - tre et Fi - li-o
sotto voce
qui cum Pa - tre et Fi - li-o
pp
ten. pp
76
si - mul a - do - ra - tur et glo -
si - mul a - do - ra - tur et glo -
pp
ten. pp
pp

81
-ri - fi - ca - tur qui lo - - cu - tus
-ri - fi - ca - tur qui lo - - cu - tus
qui lo - - cu - tus
qui lo - - cu - tus
86
est per pro - - phe - -
est per pro - - phe - -
est per pro - - phe - -
est per pro - - phe - -

91
P
ppp
tas
Et
pp
96
u - nam sanc - tam Ca - tho - li-cam
Tenore solo
Et u - nam
tho - li-cam,

100
Soprano solo
sanc - - tam Ca - tho - li-cam
Alto solo
sanc - - tam Ca - tho - li-cam et A - po -
sanc - - tam
et A - po -
Basso solo
et A - po -
104
et A - po - sto - li-cam Ec - cle - - si -
- sto - li-cam, et A - po - sto - li-cam Ec - cle - - si -
- sto - li-cam, et A - po - sto - li-cam Ec - cle - - si -
- sto - li-cam, et A - po - sto - li-cam Ec - cle - - si -

108
Tutti
f
- am,
Cre - - - - - - do,
Tutti
Tutti
Tutti
G
ff
111
Cre - - - - - - do,
con -
do, con fi - - te-or, con -

114
-fi - - te-or u - - - num bap - tis- - - - - -
-fi - - te-or u - - - num bap - tis- - - - - -
-fi - - te-or u - - - num bap - tis- - - - - -
-fi - te - or u - - - num bap - tis- - - - - -
117
-ma, Con - fi - te-or u - num bap -
-ma, Con - fi - te-or u - num bap -
-ma, Con - fi - te-or u - num bap -
-ma, Con - fi - te-or, con - fi - te - or u - num bap -

121
-tis - - - - - - -ma in re -
-tis - - - - - - -ma in re -
-tis - - - - - - -ma in re -
-tis - - - - - - - -ma in re - mis - - - si - o - nem
124
-mis - - si - o - nem pec - - ca - - to - - - - - -
-mis - - si - o - nem pec - - ca - - to - - - - - -
-mis - - si - o - nem pec - - ca - - to - - - - - -
pec - ca - to - - rum, pec - ca - to - - - - - -

127
Q
-rum
re - sur-
-rum
re - sur-rec - ti -
-rum
ex - pec - to
re - sur - rec - ti -
-rum et ex - pec - - to
re - sur - rec - ti -
3
f
3
f
130
-rec - ti - o - - - nem,
- o - - - - - nem,
- o - - - - - nem,
ex - pec - to
- o - - - - - nem, et ex - pec - - to
G
ff
f
ff
f

133
re-sur- rec - ti - o - - -nem,
re-sur-rec - ti - o - - - - - - -nem,
re - sur - rec - ti - o - - - - - - -nem,
re - sur - rec - ti - o - - - - - - -nem, re-sur-rec - ti -
136
re - sur-rec - ti -
re - sur- rec - ti - o - - nem, re - sur-rec - ti -
re - sur-rec - ti - o - - - - - nem, re - sur-rec - ti -
-o - - - - - - - - - - -nem, re - sur-rec - ti -

139
ff
-o- nem
ppp
mor- tu-
-o- nem
mor- tu-
-o- nem
mor- tu-
-o- nem
mor- tu-
ff
pp
ppp
142
-o- rum,
f
Cre-
-o- rum,
Cre-
-o- rum,
Cre-
-o- rum,
Cre-
ff
f
ff

145
-do, Cre - - - - - -do.
-do, Cre - - - - - -do.
-do, Cre - - - - - -do.
-do, Cre - - - - - -do.
ff
ff
148
151
ff
8
ff

R
155
Allegro (𝅗𝅥 = 108)
Et vi - tam ven - tu - ri sæ - cu - li A - men, A -
A -
sim.
161
men, A - men, A - men, A -
Et vi - tam ven - tu - ri sæ - cu - li
men, A - men,
A -

166
men, A - men, A -
A - men, A - men, A - men, A -
Et vi - tam ven -
men, A - men,
171
men, A - men, A -
tu - ri sæ - cu - li A - men, A -
A - men,

176
-men, A- - - men, A- - - - - - men,
-men, A- - - - - - - - - - -
-men, A- - - men, A- - - men, A- - - - -
et vi - tam ven - tu - ri sae - cu - li A - men,
181
A- - - - - - - - men, A- - - -
- - - - - - men, A - - men,
- - men, A - - men, A - - men, A- - - - -
A - - - - - men, A - - - men,
ff
ff

186
- - - - men, A- - - - - - - - -
A - - men,
- - - - - - - - men, A- - - - - - - - - - -
A- - - - - men, A- -

191
- - men, A- - - - - - - - - men,
A- - men, A- - -
- - - - men, A- - - - - - - - - - - -
- - - - men, A- - - - - - -

196
A - men, A - men, A - men, A - men,
-men, A -
-men, A -
-men, A - - men, A - - men, A -
fff
fff
201
S
A - - men, Et vi - tam ven -
- men,
- men, A -
- men, A - - men,
G

206
-tu - ri
sæ - cu - li
A - men,
A- - - - - -
A- - - - - - - men,
A-
211
-men, A- - - - men,
Et vi - tam ven - tu - ri sæ - cu - li A - men,
-men, A- - - - men,
A- - - - -
-men,
A- - - - - - - - - - -

216
A - men, A - - - -
A - - - - - - men, A - - - men, A - - men,
- men, Et vi - tam ven - tu - ri
- - - - - - men, A - - - men, A -
③
221
- - - - - - - - - men, A - -
A - - - - - - men, A - - - men,
sæ - cu - li A - men, A - - - - - men, A - -
- - - - - - - - - men, Et

226
-men, A - - - - - - men, A -
A - - - - - - - - - - -
-men, A - - - men, A - - - - - men,
vi - tam ven - tu - ri sæ - cu - li A - men, A - - -
231
- - - - men, A - -
- - - - men, A - - - - - - - - - -
A - - - men, A - - -
- - - men, A - - - - - - - men,
G

236
-men, A- - - men,
-men, A- - - - - - - - - - - - men, A- -
-men, A- - - - - - - men,
A- - - - - - - - -men, A-
241
A- -men, A- - - -men,
- - - - - - - - - - - men, A- - - - - -
A- - - - - -men, A- - - - - -
- - - - - - - - men, A- - -men,
fff
fff

246
A - men, A - men, A - men, A-
A - men, A - men,
251
men, A-
men, A-
men, A- men,A-
-men, A-
pp

257
men, A-
men,
A-
men,
262
A-
cresc.
men,
Et
f
ff

268
vi - tam ven - tu - ri sæ - cu - li A - - - men, A - - - men,
- men, et vi - tam ven - tu - ri
- men, A - - - - - men, A - - men,
- men, A - - - -
274
A - - - - - men, A - - - - - - men, A -
sæ - cu - li A - - - men, A - - - men, A - - - -
Et vi - tam ven - tu - ri sæ - cu - li A - - -
- - - - men, A - - men, et

280
T
-men, A - - - men, A - - - - - men,
-men, A - - - - - - - - - men,
-men, A - - - men, A - - - - - men.
p
vi - tam ven - tu - ri sæ - cu- li A - - - men, A - - -
pp
pp
285
cresc.
p A - - - men,
p
A - - - men, A - - - men, A - -
p
A - - men, A - - - men, A - -
men, A - - - - -
cresc.
mf

290
ff
A - men,
A - -
-men, A - men, A - men,
A - -
-men, A - - - men,
A - -
- - - - - - - men,
A - -
f
G
ff
f
ff
295
- - - men,
A - -
- - - men,
A -
- - - men, A - - - - - - - - -
- - - men, A - - - - - - - - -

299
- - - - men, A - men, A -
- - - - - - - - men, A - men, A -
- - - men, A - men, A - men, A -
- - - men, A - men, A - men, A -
303
- - men, A - - - men, A - -
- - - - - - - - - men, A - -
- - men, A - - - men, A - -
- - - - - - - - - men, A - -
fff
ff

307
men,
A
men,
A
men,
A
men,
A
311
men,
men,
pp
A
men,
pp
A
pp
men, A
pp
pp

316
pp
cresc.
A - - - - men,
-men, A- - -men, A- - - - men, A- - - -
-men, A- - - - men, A- - men,
- - - - - men, A- - - - - - - - - -
cresc.
cresc.
321
ff
A- - - - men, A- - -
-men, A - men, A- - -
A- - - - men, A- - -
- - - - men, A- - -
G
ff
ff

325
- - - - men, A- - - -
- - - - men, A- -
- - - - men, A- - - - - - - - - - - -
- - - - men, A- - - - - - - - - - - -
329
- - - men, A - men, A -
- - - men, A . - men, A - men, A -
- - - men, A - men, A - men, A -
- - - men, A - men, A - men, A -

men, A - men, A
men, A
men, A - men, A
men, A

men, A
men, A
men, A
men, A

341
men,
men,
men,
men, A
345
A- men, A- men, A- men,
A- men, A- men, A
A- men, A - men,
men, A - men
A-

349
A - - men, A - - - men, A - - - men,
- - men, A - - - men, A - - - men,
-men, A - - - men, A - - - - - - - - men,
-men, A - - - men, A - men, A - men,
353
ff
A - - - men, A - - - - - - -
A - - - men, A - - - - - - -
A - - - men, A - - - - - - -
A - - - men, A - - - - - - -
fff

358
U
- - - - - men.
- - - - - men.
- - - - - men.
- - - - - men.
pp
364
Soprano solo
sotto voce
In u- - num De- - um
Alto solo
sotto voce
In u- - num De- - um
Tenore solo
sotto voce
In u- - num De- - um
Basso solo
sotto voce
In u- - num De- - um
ppp
pppp

370
Tutti
Tempo I
ff
Cre - - - - - - - - - do.
Tutti
ff
Cre - - - - - - - - - do.
Tutti
ff
Cre - - - - - - - - - do.
Tutti
ff
Cre - - - - - - - - - do.
G
ff
Tempo I
ff
375
ff
ff
379
ff
fff
ff

11. Preludio religioso

(Offertorium)

32
37
42
47
52
57
p
f
p
pp
cresc.
f
ff
f

62
f
67
ff
pp
72
77
82
cresc.
87
p
pp una corda

92
cresc.
97
f
ff
102
p
p
107
f
f
ff
112
ff
pp
pp
117
ppp
cresc.

rall. un poco
in tempo
rit.
in tempo
cresc.
rit.
in tempo
cresc.
Klavier
Tempo I

Ritornello

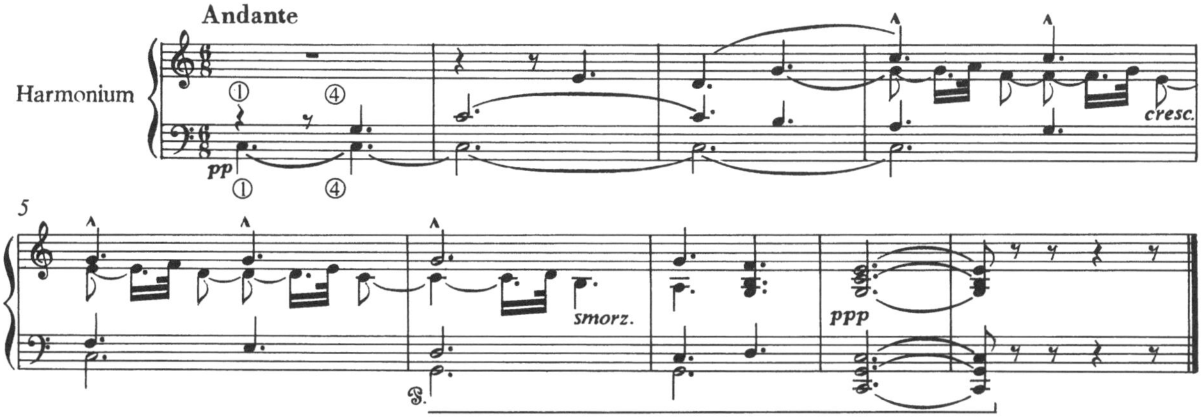

12. Sanctus

Soli und Chor

Andantino mosso

10
Tutti
Ple - ni sunt coe - li et ter - ra glo - ri - a tu - a.
coe - li et ter - ra glo - ri - a tu - a. Solo Ho - san - na in ex -
ter - ra glo - ri - a, glo - ri - a tu - a
- ra glo - ri - a, glo - ri - a tu - a. Solo Ho - san - na in ex -
14
Solo Ho - san - na in ex - cel - sis Tutti sotto voce Be - ne -
- cel - sis Tutti sotto voce Be - ne -
Solo Ho - san - na in ex - cel - sis Tutti sotto voce Be - ne -
- cel - sis Tutti sotto voce Be - ne -
19
- dic - tus, Be - ne - dic - tus qui ve - nit,
- dic - tus, Be - ne - dic - tus qui ve - nit,
- dic - tus, Be - ne - dic - tus qui ve - nit,
- dic - tus, Be - ne - dic - tus qui ve - nit,

ve - nit in no-mi-ne Do - mi - ni,
Ple-ni sunt coeli et
ve - nit in no-mi-ne Do - mi - ni,
Ple-ni sunt coe-li et ter - ra
ve - nit in no-mi-ne Do - mi - ni,
Ple-ni sunt coeli et ter - ra glo-ri- a,
ve - nit in no-mi-ne Do - mi - ni,
Ple-ni sunt coe-li et ter - - ra glo-ri- a,
ter - ra glo-ri - a tu - a
Solo
Ho - san - na in ex -
glo - ri - a tu - a
Solo
Ho- san - na in ex - cel - sis
glo - ri - a tu - a
Solo
Ho- san - na in ex -
glo - ri - a tu - a
Solo
Ho- san - na in ex - cel - sis
- cel - - sis
Tutti
sotto voce
Be - ne - - dic - tus, Be - ne -
Tutti
sotto voce
Be - ne - - dic - tus, Be - ne -
- cel - - sis
Tutti
sotto voce
Be - ne - - dic - tus, Be - ne -
Tutti
sotto voce
Be - ne - - dic - tus, Be - ne -

38
-dic - - tus qui ve - nit, ve - - nit in no-mi-ne Do - mi -
-dic - - tus qui ve - nit, ve - - nit in no-mi-ne Do - mi -
-dic - - tus qui ve - nit, ve - - nit in no-mi-ne Do - mi -
-dic - - tus qui ve - - nit, ve - - nit in no-mi-ne Do - mi -
42
Solo ppp
- ni, qui ve-nit in no-mi-ne Do-mi - - ni, qui ve-nit in
- ni, qui ve-nit in no-mi-ne Do-mi - - ni, qui ve-nit in
- ni, in no-mi-ne Do-mi - - ni, qui ve-nit in
Solo pp
- ni, qui ve-nit in no - - mi - ne Do-mi - - ni, qui ve-nit in
46
Tutti
no-mi-ne Do - mi - ni, in no - - mi - ne Do - mi - ni,
no-mi-ne Do - mi - ni, no - - mi - ne Do - mi - ni,
no-mi-ne Do - mi - ni, no - - mi - ne Do - mi - ni,
Solo
no-mi-ne Do - mi - ni, no - - mi - ne Do - mi - ni, qui ve-nit in

50
Solo ppp
qui ve- nit in no-mi - ne Do-mi - ni, qui ve- nit in no-mi - ne Do - mi -
Solo ppp
qui ve- nit in no-mi - ne Do-mi - ni, qui ve- nit in no-mi - ne Do - mi -
Solo ppp
in no-mi - ne Do-mi - ni, qui ve- nit in no-mi - ne Do - mi -
no- - mi - ne Do-mi - ni, qui ve- nit in no-mi - ne Do - mi -
54
Tutti ppp
- ni, in no- - mi - ne Do - mi - ni Ho-san - na, Ho-san -
Tutti ppp
- ni, no- - mi - ne Do - mi - ni Ho-san - na, Ho-san -
Tutti ppp
- ni, no- - mi - ne Do - mi - ni Ho-san - na, Ho-san -
Tutti ppp
- ni, no- - mi - ne Do - mi - ni Ho-san - na, Ho-san -
pp
ff
58
- na, Ho-san - na in ex - cel - sis.
- na, Ho-san - na in ex - cel-sis, ex - cel - sis.
- na, Ho-san - na in ex - cel-sis, ex - cel - sis.
in ex cel-sis, ex - cel - sis.
- na, Ho-san - na in ex - cel - sis.

13. O salutaris hostia

Sopran solo

ho - - sti - a Quæ cœ - li pan - - - dis o - - - - sti -
- um, quæ cœ - li pan - dis, quæ cœ - li pan - - -
- - - dis o - - - sti - um.
Animando un pochino
Bel - - la pre - munt ho - sti - - li - a Bel - - la pre - munt ho -
- sti - - li - a da ro - bur fer au - xi - - li - um,

60
da ro - bur fer au - xi - li - um, da ro - bur fer au -
66
ff
ff
pppp
- xi - - li - um, da ro - bur fer au - xi - - -
71
ritornando al tempo I°
- - - li - um,
78
X
f
p
O sa - lu - ta - ris ho - - sti - a Quæ cœ - li pan - - dis o -
84
f
- - sti - um, O sa - lu - ta - ris ho - - sti - a quæ

90
cæ - li pan - - dis o - - - sti - - um.
pp
95
Bel - - la pre - munt, pre - munt,
100
pre - munt, pre - munt ho - sti - li - - a
f
105
cresc.
da ro - bur, da ro - bur, da ro - bur
ppp
cresc.
111
f
fer au - xi - li - - um, da ro - bur fer au - - xi - li -
f
smorz.

117
Y
-um, da ro - - bur fer au - xi - li - um.
pp
f
123
Bel - la pre-munt ho - sti - li - a,
ff
f
128
Bel - la pre-munt ho - sti - li - a,
Bel - la pre-munt ho -
ff
134
-sti - li - a
da ro - bur,
p
pp
ppp
140
cresc.
da ro - bur, da ro - bur fer au - xi - li -
cresc.
f

146
-um, da ro-bur fer au- - xi - li - - um, da ro - -
smorz.
pp
152
- bur fer au - xi - - li - - um
pp
pppp
158
A - - men,
A - -
164
- - men.
169
ff

14. Agnus Dei

Alto solo und Chor

De - - - i qui tol - - - lis pec-ca-ta mun - - di, qui tol - - - lis pec-ca-ta
mun - - - di mi - - se - - re - - - re mi - se-re - re
no - - - bis, qui tol - lis pec - - - ca - - - ta, pec - ca - ta

17
pp
mun - - di mi - se - re - re, mi - se - - re - re no - - -
ppp
pp
19
- bis
Soprani
sotto voce
Do - na no - bis pa - cem, do - na no - bis pa - cem
Alti
sotto voce
Do - na no - bis pa - cem, do - na no - bis pa - cem
CORO
Tenori
sotto voce
Do - na no - bis pa - cem, do - na no - bis pa - cem
Bassi
sotto voce
Do - na no - bis pa - cem, do - na no - bis pa - cem
Z
21
Alto solo
dolce
A - - gnus
pppp
ppp

23
De- - - i qui tol- - - lis peccata mun- - - di, qui tol- - - lis peccata
25
mun- - - di mi- - - se- - - re- - - - re, mi - se-re - re
27
no- - - - - bis, qui tol- - lis pec- -

28
ff
- - - ca - - - - - - ta, pec - ca - ta
f
f
29
pp
mun - di mi - se - re - re, mi - se - re - re no - -
pppp
ppp
31
- bis
CORO
Soprani
sotto voce
Do - na no - bis pa - cem, do - na no - bis pa - cem
Alti
sotto voce
Do - na no - bis pa - cem, do - na no - bis pa - cem
Tenori
sotto voce
Do - na no - bis pa - cem, do - na no - bis pa - cem
Bassi
sotto voce
Do - na no - bis pa - cem, do - na no - bis pa - cem

33
Aa
Alto solo
dolce
A - - - gnus
pppp
ppp
35
3
f
De - - - i qui tol - - lis peccata mun - - di, qui tol - - lis pecca-ta
37
pp
mun - - - di do - - - na no - - bis pa - - - -

39
-cem, do- - na no- - -bis pa- - - - -
sim.
41
-cem, do- - - na no- - - bis, do- - - na
f
43
no- - -bis, do- - - na, do- - na no-bis pa- - -
④
pp

45
-cem
Soprani
sotto voce
Do - na no - bis pa - cem, do - na no - bis pa-
Alti
sotto voce
Do - na no - bis pa - cem, do - na no - bis pa-
CORO
Tenori
sotto voce
Do - na no - bis pa - cem, do - na no - bis pa-
Bassi
sotto voce
Do - na no - bis pa - cem, do - na no - bis pa-
47
Alto solo
p
Qui tol - lis pec - ca -
-cem, qui tol - lis pec - ca - ta,
-cem, qui tol - lis pec -
-cem, qui tol - lis pec - ca - ta,
-cem. qui tol - lis pec - ca -
④
ppp
④
ppp

49
cresc.
rinforz.
- ta, pec - ca - ta mun - di mi-se-re - re, mi-se-
pec - ca - ta mun - - - - di
- ca - ta, pec - ca - ta mun - di
pec - ca - ta mun - di
- ta, pec - ca - ta mun - di
G
51
f
- re - - re, mi - - se - re - - - - re

52
no- - - - - bis, do - na no- - - bis pa- - - - -
do- - - - - na no - bis pa- - - - -
do- - - - - na no - bis pa- - - - -
do- - - - - na no - bis pa- - - - -
do- - - - - na no - bis pa- - - - -
53
-cem, qui tol- - - lis pec-ca- - -
-cem, qui tol- - - lis pec - ca- - - ta,
-cem, qui tol - lis pec-
-cem, qui tol- - - - lis pec - ca- - - - - ta,
-cem, qui tol- - - - - - lis pec - ca- - - - -

55
cresc.
rinf.
-ta, pec-ca-ta mun-di, mi-se-re-re, mi-se-
pec-ca-ta mun-di
-ca-ta, pec-ca-ta mun-di
pec-ca-ta mun-di
-ta, pec-ca-ta mun-di
G
cresc.
rinf.
cresc.
rinf.
57
f
-re-re, mi-se-re-re
f
f

Bb
tutta forza
58
ff
no - - - - - bis, do - - - - - - -na
Soprani
do - na no - bis, do - na no - bis,
Alti
do - na no - bis, do - na no - bis,
Tenori
do - na no - bis, do - na no - bis,
Bassi
do - na no - bis, do - na no - bis,
ff tutta forza
59
no - - - - bis pa - - - - - - - -
do - na no - bis pa - - - - - - - -
do - na no - bis pa - - - - - - - -
do - na no - bis pa - - - - - - - -
do - na no - bis pa - - - - - - - -

60
-cem.
-cem.
-cem.
-cem.
-cem.
tutta forza
tutta forza
62
ppp
p
66
tutti registri
ff
fff
ff
mf
ff
f
ff
fff